5 TIPS...

BECOME A SUCCESSFUL PUBLISHED AUTHOR

Bethany Kelly

women lead
PUBLISHING™

TABLE OF CONTENTS

A MESSAGE FROM THE AUTHOR

Books are in my bones.

I have fond childhood memories of being in my family's print shop. I remember the sound the offset printer made as it clanked and chugged along. The rich scent of freshly printed paper with its still-wet ink. The red light of the darkroom and the acrid chemicals in the development baths.

I'd watch with fascination as printing plates were made, as the press operator meticulously adjusted multiple dials to get things just so, as hulking machines strained and thumped as they collated, folded, stitched, or stapled papers together to create books.

I love books. I love holding a book up to my face and inhaling its scent. Sure, I own a Kindle device, but something about turning a physical book's pages gives me a feeling of satisfaction. Curling up with a good book on a rainy day is my idea of a good time. So is lying outside on a beautiful day with a new book. I read anywhere from two to four books each month, and that doesn't count the books I read as part of my work. I devour all types of books, but memoir is my favorite genre. I love reading true stories about real people.

I've been involved in production and publishing in one way or another for my entire career. I love what I do, and I can't believe I am so lucky that I get to work every day with authors who are publishing their books. I love participating in the creation of a new book. When I hold that finished book in my hand for the first time, the knowledge that "I helped make that" fills me with joy.

It seems only natural that my own foray into becoming an author is a book on the topic of publishing. In this book we will wind through the general trajectory one takes when writing and publishing a book. I will give you my best tips, tips I have gathered over years of doing this work. This isn't a comprehensive how-to book. There are many other books like that, and I recommend many of them.

This book is intended to be a short, easy read that gives you an overview of what goes into the process. My hope is that it inspires you that you can do this! You can become a successful, published author. It's doable. It's absolutely possible for you. The secret is to put one foot in front of the other and keep taking steps down the publishing path. Publishing is a journey of many steps, and I'd like to think that reading this book is the first step you are taking on your own publishing journey.

COME UP WITH A CONCEPT THAT SELLS

1

Define what success as an author means to you

● ● ●

People publish for a variety of reasons. What is yours? How do you see this book impacting your life, career, or legacy? What's in it for you? Determine from the very beginning what your personal motivation is and what your goal is in writing a book. Think of what you want this book to do for *you*. Are you looking to increase your credibility, expand your reach, tell your story, get speaking engagements or stand out from other experts in your field? Getting clear on this will inform your decision-making and choices moving forward. It's OK. Be selfish for a moment.

Figure out who your audience will be

● ● ●

If you hope to write a book for everyone, you will speak to no one. You want to get as clear as you can about who your audience is. Continue to narrow down your audience until it is as specific as you can get. Your audience could be women, but can you make it more specific? Mothers? Businesswomen? Drill down even further. Stay-at-home moms or women who are solopreneurs? The clearer you can get about your audience, the more relevant your book will be in the marketplace.

Uncover what your audience's struggle is

●　●　●

You want to identify what your audience struggles with.
What keeps them up at night? What are they worried about?
When you are an expert in an area, you get the big picture: you
know what your audience *needs* in order to solve their problem.
But readers will only care about what you have to say if they
feel you understand their problem. So get really clear about
what that problem is.

4

Find out where your book fits into the existing market

● ● ●

Imagine your book on a shelf in the bookstore. What shelf would it be on? What other books are in the same genre as yours? Narrowing down your book's genre gives you more focus and clarity. Write a book that fits into an existing audience base so you don't have to build that base from scratch. Plus, each genre has its own conventions. Your audience will expect certain things out of particular types of books. You want to understand your audience clearly so you can deliver what they want and need.

5

Dig around in the existing market to uncover what is missing

●　●　●

While you want your book to fit into an existing market, you also want to stand out in that market. There must be something different about your book or the approach you take that no one else is talking about. A good way to figure this out is to buy three to five best-selling books similar to the book you want to write. Read them and note what they aren't covering at all or aren't covering well. Find the hole in the market only you can fill.

6

Articulate how you are uniquely qualified to address that problem

● ● ●

There is something about you that makes you the right person to address the struggle your audience faces. Is it your experience? Perhaps it's your education. You may think anyone could write about your subject, but that is not true. You will bring something unique to the topic that no one else can. Discover, or uncover, what that is. It will motivate you and give you the confidence you need.

7

Scour Amazon's user reviews on books that are similar to yours

• • •

Amazon's user reviews are a gold mine for uncovering what your audience expects, values, and needs in a book in your genre or on your topic. Scour the user reviews on the books you have chosen that are similar to yours. Take note of what people found valuable in the book and especially what they felt was missing or not covered well. You'll get good ideas for what readers want that you can focus on in your book, especially when that is not being delivered in similar books.

SET YOURSELF UP FOR SUCCESS IN WRITING

Determine if you need short, focused time or larger blocks of time to write

●   ●   ●

Understanding what works for you in terms of productive, creative time will help you arrange your schedule. Some people do their best work when they have short, focused daily time to write—thirty minutes to an hour. Others need longer periods of time to work. It may take them longer to get "in the groove"—but once they are there, they can stay in it for a long time. Daylong periods or weekends away can be optimal. If you aren't sure what works best for you, try each of them and see what feels right.

Block out time in your schedule to write

● ● ●

You will never "find" the time to write. You have to make time. A book is written one word at a time, and the only way to get those words on the page is to spend time at it. Let's say you can put 500 words on the page in a single writing session. You would need 40 sessions to produce 20,000 words. Let's say you schedule three sessions a week. Within three months, you could have your entire first draft done. See how doable it is? Now, go schedule your writing time!

10

Create an initial outline

• • •

It doesn't have to be a traditional outline. You can start with a list of topics and subtopics, or you can create a mind map (a diagram used to organize information visually). Creating an initial outline or a list of topics will help guide you as you begin to write. Don't spend a lot of time on your outline. It doesn't need to be perfect because, as you write the book, the outline *will* change. But starting with an initial framework gives you a way to measure progress as you write your first draft.

11

Start with a "brain dump"

● ● ●

The goal for your first draft is to get your ideas and thoughts out of your head and onto the page. I call this the brain dump. Don't edit or organize during the brain dump. In fact, the faster you can go, the better. You want to bypass the "perfectionist" part of your brain and engage the creative side. Set a timer and type everything and anything that comes to your mind on a certain topic. When the timer goes off, save and close the file. When your next writing session comes along, open the file, go to the end, set the timer, and start in where you left off.

12

Refine your content

• • •

Once your brain dump is finished, go back and refine the rest of your content. You want to consider clarity. Is what you are saying making sense? This is where you think about organization, too. Is the material presented in a way that makes sense for the reader? There will be a fair bit of rewriting and reorganization during this phase. While the brain dump got your ideas down on paper, the refining stage allows you to massage the content with the reader in mind and get it to where you want it to be.

13

Make sure each chapter is structured well

● ● ●

You want each chapter to have a beginning, a middle and an end. Start each chapter with a powerful sentence that draws readers in and makes them want to keep reading. End each chapter with a sentence that makes readers want to turn the page and start the next chapter. Give some thought as to what elements you want each chapter to have, then make sure there is consistency throughout. (Chapter elements could include: a title, a quote, a callout, footnotes, subheadings, bullet points, lists, action steps.)

14

Do a final read for continuity and flow

• • •

Before you consider yourself "finished" with your book and ready to take the next step, go through your manuscript a final time with a focus on making certain the flow works as a whole. You want to make sure the content fits together well, overall. Look at the overall order of chapters and the flow of information. Think of a necklace of pearls. Are the pearls strung together in a way that presents a polished, final picture? Will the presentation of the material make sense to an uninitiated reader? Some reorganization of chapters may be necessary.

15

Don't forget to add front and end matter

• • •

It's easy to forget about front and end matter when you are finalizing your manuscript. Front and end matter are finishing touches. They give a book that professional feel. Front and end matter are things like:

- Title page
- Copyright page
- Dedication
- Table of contents
- Acknowledgements
- End notes/footnotes
- Additional resources / recommended reading
- About the author

Choose front and end matter relevant to your book. Check out books in a similar genre to see what type of front and end matter are appropriate.

TAKE CHARGE OF THE PUBLISHING PROCESS

16

Transform yourself from a writer into a publisher

● ● ●

In order to successfully self-publish, once you are finished writing, you need to take off the hat of an author and put on the hat of a publisher. Writing and publishing are both important roles, but very different skill sets are involved. As the publisher, you will be tasked with organizing the production and publishing process. You become the one who makes the decisions. You will be managing all the moving parts and pieces of the production, and you will be responsible for the marketing and promotion.

17

Learn what you need to learn in order to become a good publisher

● ● ●

If this is your first book, there will be plenty for you to learn. The good news is that all of the information you need is available and easily accessible. A good rule of thumb is: the more overall understanding you have, the better decisions you will be able to make. Publishing isn't rocket science. Everything is learnable. So do your research. Read. Ask questions. Educate yourself.

18

Become the leader of your publishing process

●　●　●

You will need to make many decisions throughout the course of your publishing journey. Take leadership of the process. This is your book, and final decisions should always be yours. Get the advice and support you need, but remember that any decision you make should be based on what you believe is best for you personally as the author, as well as what is best for your book.

19

Choose the level of quality you want for your book

• • •

This is an important decision to make early on, because it will inform the decisions that follow. Is your priority to put a book together quickly, so you can get it out in the world as soon as possible? Or is your goal to create a high-quality book you will be proud of forever? There is no right or wrong way to publish a book. But you need a clear vision of what you want to accomplish because it will determine the direction you take going forward.

20

Get help from professionals

• • •

If you plan to create a high-quality book, you will want to get help from professionals (like an editor, designer, an e-book formatter, perhaps an illustrator). Your job will be to choose competent professionals to work with, contract with them in a way that works for both of you, and communicate with them so they understand what you need. These are all roles the publisher handles.

21

As the publisher, keep things moving and on track

● ● ●

You will need to manage a lot of moving parts and pieces during the publishing process. The job of the publisher is to keep things on track, to keep things moving from one step to the next. Don't let your project lose momentum or get stuck. While the writing process can be grueling and time-consuming, the publishing process can move quickly and with a good deal of momentum if you keep things on track. Keeping the publisher mind-set helps you avoid drowning in the details.

22

Get someone else to manage the publishing process for you

●　●　●

If you don't have the inclination or the time to learn what you need to know about the publishing process and manage it well, you can get someone else to handle this. Author services companies handle these types of tasks. My company, Publishing Partner, is brilliant at managing the publishing process and focuses on all the production pieces that are needed, from design to ebook, to getting you visible on Amazon. You will still want to be the leader of your publishing process, but a professional who manages the production process—including bringing quality professionals to the table—can take a load off of you as the author.

AFTER THE WRITING
... COMES THE
EDITING

23

Don't write in an echo chamber

● ● ●

An author can become so immersed in her subject that it is impossible to see things—important things—that someone not as close to the topic will be able to see. Someone else's perspective on the material you have written can show up holes or missing bits of information. It's a great way to "test" your material to see how it is received and if it is understood. Two ways to do this are through beta readers or a developmental edit. Get feedback from others.

24

Choose a few beta readers

• • •

Beta readers are individuals who agree to read your book in advance of it being published. Typically beta readers are not professional editors, but they should be knowledgeable or interested in the topic you are writing about. Ask these individuals to give you feedback as to anything that is missing or unclear. Ask them to comment on whether the tone or voice of the material works for them. As the author, you can choose whether or not to implement changes based on their feedback, but you will gain useful insight from their comments.

25

A developmental edit can be useful

• • •

A developmental edit is typically done by a professional editor, who looks at the big picture of the book and gives you feedback and suggestions for improvement. They look at how the content can be improved. Here is what a developmental editor will evaluate:

- The strength and presentation of the content (including what might be missing that should be added or what might be better taken away)
- The structure and organization of the content (Does the structure work? Is the story arc strong?)
- The style (including voice, tone, etc.)
- The reader's perspective (does it grab and keep the reader's attention?)

26

Pay for a professional copyeditor

• • •

Every manuscript needs a copyedit. The job of a copyeditor is to make sure your manuscript is correct. Accuracy is their focus. They will correct grammar, punctuation, tenses, improve awkward sentences, fact check and look for inconsistencies. A copyeditor will focus on a host of grammatical details in order to make the manuscript work. A good copyedit is one way to circumvent the stigma that can be attached to poorly produced self-published books. So pay for a good editor. You'll thank me later.

27

Proofreading is a good plan

• • •

The best time for a proofread is after the book has been designed, and a proofread should be done on paper. Ideally you want someone proofreading who hasn't read the book before and can see it with fresh eyes. A proofread catches mistakes or errors—in content or formatting—that may have eluded you. (It happens, especially when all previous readings of the book have been done on a screen.) Adding a proofread as a final step is a good way to ensure that you won't be embarrassed by a typo once the book is in print.

28

For the highest-quality outcome, choose two other options besides copyedit

● ● ●

A copyedit is a must. And in addition, I recommend an author choose at least two of the three other options presented in this section: either beta readers or a developmental edit along with a proofread. Doing this will ensure that you have had enough eyes on your book to show up any flaws or imperfections. Implementing the feedback you get will make your book as strong as it can be and a pleasure to read.

29

Ask for what you want so you get what you need

● ● ●

Understanding the various types of editing that are available will help you make a clear request. Whether you are paying for a service, or asking a friend, family member or colleague to help you out, you want to be specific about the type of feedback you are looking for. For example, if you ask a well-read family member to proofread your book, explain that you are only looking for errors. You wouldn't want them to spend their time making helpful editing suggestions because that is not what you need at the proofreading stage.

When evaluating whether an editor is suitable, ask for a sample edit

• • •

Prior to officially engaging a copyeditor, you can request a sample edit of at least a page or two. A sample edit will show you the types of changes a copyeditor will make. If you have more than one potential candidate, having both do a copyedit can help you evaluate who is the best fit for your book, your content, and your voice.

BOOK COVERS
AND STYLE

31

People *do* judge a book by its cover.
So find a professional to help you
design yours

• • •

Think of your cover as an important piece of marketing.
A good cover will inspire the reader to pick up the book (or
click the thumbnail online to learn more about it). This is what
you want and need. Unless you are a professional designer, it
is worth spending the money to get one to design your cover.

32

Contract with a designer whose overall style you like

• • •

Look over a potential designer's cover portfolio before signing a contract. Every designer has his or her own style, and that style will typically be evident across a range of covers. You should like the individual's overall style. Find out if the designer is experienced in creating covers for the type of book you are writing. Fiction covers have different design needs than nonfiction. Some designers cross over well; others don't.

Make sure you understand what is included in the price

● ● ●

When you are communicating with a potential designer regarding price, make sure you understand everything that is included. How many concepts will he or she present you with? How long can you expect each stage to take? Can you request changes? If so, how many rounds of changes are included in the price? A designer will typically accommodate your changes but might charge extra for it. Understanding all the costs upfront is a smart move on your part.

34

Create a design brief to give to the designer

• • •

A design brief is a document that includes all the information a designer needs to start creating a cover. Important things to include:

- The title (and subtitle)
- Your name as you wish it to appear on the cover
- Genre (what type of book: fiction, self-help, business, financial)
- Trim size (the size of the book)
- Book type (paperback, hardback, e-book)
- What printing solution you are using (CreateSpace, IngramSpark, offset printer)

35

Help the designer out by doing your own cover research

• • •

Look at existing covers in your genre. You can take a trip to a bookstore or spend some time on Amazon. Take photos or save the links of covers you like. Include reference book cover images in the design brief. If you can explain why you like the reference covers, that is even better. Also include some that you *don't* like, and explain why if you can. This will allow the designer to learn a lot about your preferences and style, and make it easier to come up with a winning cover you love.

36

Give the designer a few concept ideas to start with

• • •

Think of a few ideas of how your cover could look, and share them with the designer in the design brief. It's best not to get too attached to any concept idea, because a designer will often come up with something really great you wouldn't have thought you would like. But a few ideas can give the designer something to start with or to use as a springboard.

TO AMAZON
AND BEYOND

37

Make your book available on Amazon

• • •

Amazon has a huge customer base (around 100 million Prime members in the United States alone). Amazon can get your book in front of potential buyers you would be hard-pressed to find on your own. The good news for an author is that if you present your book in a way that ticks all the right boxes for Amazon, Amazon's complex algorithm machine will go to work on your behalf and start pushing your book to its customers. Services like CreateSpace, Kindle Direct Publishing, and IngramSpark make it simple to get your book on Amazon.

38

Set up your author page on Amazon

● ● ●

Amazon provides each author with a complimentary author profile page. This is another way your readers can find and connect with you. On the author profile page, readers can learn more about you, easily see all of your books (if you have more than one book), and find your website and blog (if you have a blog). Take advantage of this opportunity to build your author platform by claiming the page and setting it up with all the available features.

Plan a book launch

● ● ●

Your book is brand-new only once, so it's appropriate to get excited and make a big deal out of the fact that it is ready to launch. The goals of a launch are to tell as many people as you can that the book is ready, generate buzz and excitement, and inspire people to buy it. You can plan an online launch, an offline launch, or both. It can be a celebratory event or a strategic, business-based event. Design a launch that supports your uniqueness and the goals you have for the book.

40

Host a party where your friends and family can celebrate with you (and buy the book)

● ● ●

You deserve to celebrate that your book is finished. Not everyone can call themselves an author, because not everyone is willing to go through all the work to write and publish a book. You did it! Now have a party and celebrate. It can be as simple or elaborate as you wish, but invite your friends, family, colleagues, and coworkers. It's a great opportunity to thank those whose support made it possible, and it's a fabulous way to make a splash with your book. Plus you can sell copies of your book at the party.

41

Get curious about where your readers already gather

● ● ●

The goal is to find as many readers as possible and get your book in front of them. No matter what genre your book is, I guarantee you there are places online or offline where your readers already gather around the general topic of your book. Get curious. Look online for existing groups, forum discussions, blogs, podcasts, influencers. Look offline for Meetup groups, clubs, gathering spots, magazines, newspapers, etc. Think outside of the box too. Ask yourself: where would people interested in this topic go to find other people interested in this topic?

Make a plan for getting your book in front of new readers

• • •

Once you've found out where your readers gather, the next step is to create a master plan that gets your book in front of those readers. Don't limit yourself to what people say is "done" or not. Also, strategize with a time frame in mind. What are some simple goals you can achieve easily? Do those first. What plans will be worthwhile but may take time and energy to achieve? Start with what's simple and take steps toward the actions that need more effort and will take longer.

43

Develop your social media presence one platform at a time

● ● ●

Social media is a great way to promote your book. The challenge is the number of platforms available. For example: Facebook, Twitter, Instagram, blogs, YouTube, Pinterest. When you are just starting out, the sheer volume of available options can be overwhelming and can paralyze you, preventing you from doing anything. It's unrealistic to expect to be active on every platform. A better choice is to pick one platform (two, tops) and strategically develop your presence on that platform. Consistency is key. And consistency is impossible to achieve if you spread yourself over too many social media platforms.

44

Create a higher-priced offering you can bundle with the book

● ● ●

All book sales are good. But there is a ceiling to how much you can charge per book, and a limit to how much a reader will be able to implement what you write about in your book. Can you leverage your skill set and knowledge by creating an offering that gives your readers more, and that you can charge more for? Consider creating a workshop, training program (in-person or online), webinar series, or even a certification program.

45

Take advantage of your status as an author to get speaking engagements

● ● ●

A great way to get your book in front of new readers is to speak to your target audience. Speaking allows your audience to quickly develop a relationship with you that generates interest in your book. A speaking engagement doesn't have to be you speaking on a stage in front of hundreds of people (although it could be). You can also speak on a podcast, radio show, author Q&A, or industry event. You can actively seek out speaking opportunities or simply remain on the lookout and be ready to say yes to any that come to you.

SHAMELESS
SELF-PROMOTION

46

Tell everyone you meet that you are an author

● ● ●

Now that you have a book published, the title of author should become part of who you are, part of the lexicon that describes you. Not everyone can call themselves an author because not everyone is willing to invest their time and energy (and in many cases money) in order to publish a book. Not everyone who wants or tries to write a book makes it across the finish line. The fact you have done so is something to be proud of! You deserve the title of author. Get comfortable with it and start using it—everywhere and with everyone.

47

Get comfortable becoming your book's number one promoter

●　●　●

Many newly minted authors are hesitant, shy or fearful about putting themselves out there and promoting their book. Imagine that your best friend just published a book. You think your friend's book is excellent, and you are determined to support your friend in getting her book out into the world. How would you be? Whom would you tell? What would you say? How would you say it? Do the same for your own book, and you will step into the role of being your book's number one fan and its number one promoter. You owe this to yourself and your book.

48

Develop a short verbal description you use to tell everyone about your book

● ● ●

In it, you'll obviously include what the book is about. But, especially in the case of nonfiction books, you'll also include who the book is for and what problem it solves. For example: "I've written a book called ____. It's a book for soon-to-be-divorced moms, full of great advice on how to get through the divorce process while remaining sane, and protecting their own interests and the needs of their children." When you are this specific, the individual you are telling will know immediately whether she is your target reader. If so, you have just made a potential sale!

49

Always keep a few copies of your book with you or in your car

• • •

Make sure you always have easy access to your book, so you have it readily available when someone expresses interest, and you can give or sell that person a copy. Keep some copies in your purse, backpack, or office tote. Keep a few copies in your desk at work or in the trunk of your car.

50

Every time someone tells you they like your book, ask them to leave a review on Amazon

● ● ●

The more reviews you have on Amazon, the better. Reviews provide social proof to other readers that your book is being read and enjoyed. Also, a quantity of reviews—especially current reviews—triggers Amazon's algorithms in a way that makes your book more visible to other readers. Think about how many books you have personally reviewed. Not so many, right? So plan on asking for the reviews you need. A review does not have to be long. Something as simple as "I enjoyed this book" works.

51

Create a simple card or postcard that promotes your book, and hand it out to potential readers

• • •

Create a simple postcard or business card that is specifically focused on your book. You can use services such as Vistaprint or MOO. At a minimum, include an image of the book cover, your contact information and your website or the book's website. If the book is available on Amazon, say so. Give this card to anyone who expresses interest in your book. A card like this can remind an interested reader about your book after your in-person interaction has passed. It will provide the information needed to find and buy your book later.

52

Create simple images using quotes from your book, and use them to promote your book on social media

● ● ●

An eye-catching image is a great way to promote your book on social media. And you don't have to be a designer to create a simple image. Since you just wrote a book, you'll have plenty of material you can pull short quotes from. Use an app like Canva or Word Swag to create simple graphic images with your quotes that you can post on social media. Along with the graphic, make sure to post your name, the title of your book, and the link to where it can be purchased.

ADDITIONAL RESOURCES

Recommended books

How to Write a Book That Sells You: Increase Your Credibility, Income, and Impact by Robin Colucci. This is the book you want to read when you are in the planning stages. Robin shows you how to turn your book idea into a sellable concept, what type of book and organizational structure will work best for your book and you as an author, and how to connect with your target audience.

Self-Publishing Boot Camp Guide for Authors, 4th Edition: Your roadmap to creating, publishing, promoting, and selling your books by Carla S King. If you are going the self-publishing route, this book is a must-have. A comprehensive guide on everything you need to know to publish professionally and successfully. Includes electronic updates.

How to Sell Books by the Truckload on Amazon!: Master Amazon and Sell More Books! By Penny C Sansevieri. When you want to understand what works on Amazon, this is the book to read. Penny shows you how to position your book to increase your visibility and sales.

Online Resources

Joel Friedlander at www.thebookdesigner.com

Joel Friedlander has published a voluminous amount of high-quality content on his website and blog that is designed to support authors. Articles, templates, and toolkits abound. I recommend two specific resources:

His book-design templates are a fantastic resource for the author who is going the DIY route: www.bookdesigntemplates.com

His monthly ebook cover-design awards, a great way to get educated on good vs. bad cover design as you read through a professional's critique on multiple covers. You'll get examples in real life of what works for cover design, what doesn't, and why.

The Hot Sheet at www.hotsheetpub.com

The Hot Sheet is a subscription-based, bimonthly publishing industry email newsletter for authors. It keeps you up to date and informed on what is going on in the industry. It offers context, perspective, analysis, and news that impacts the industry. The information helps you stay on top of news and relevant trends, and synthesizes a lot of information into an easy-to-read format.

●   ●   ●

Other Resources

**Independent Book Publishers Association at
www.ibpa-online.org**

The IBPA is a tremendous resource for current or future authors, publishers (independent and hybrid), and those affiliated with the publishing industry. The association offers its members business services, education, legal services, publishing resources, magazine subscriptions, networking, etc.

* * *

ABOUT THE AUTHOR

Bethany Kelly is the founder and CEO of Publishing Partner, a successful author services business. Bethany turns experts into authors and supports the busy professional in getting his or her book projects finished. She is passionate about creating beautiful, brilliant books. Her clients are primarily business professionals publishing under their own imprint. In its first five years of existence, Publishing Partner supported authors in completing close to 50 titles. Many of her authors have become Amazon #1 best sellers. A few of them have ranked in the top 100 in their category for several months.

She is also a founding partner and the managing editor of Women Lead Publishing, a publishing company that gives voice, credibility and influence to female authors enabling them to step into an expanded role of thought-leadership and impact through published works.

With over 20 years of experience in the publishing industry, she brings her expertise and warmth to each author she works with. When you work with Bethany, you can be sure of three things:

- Your project will get finished.
- It will be high quality (content and presentation).
- You'll have a good experience becoming an author.

Learn more at www.publishingpartner.com

ABOUT WOMEN LEAD PUBLISHING

Women Lead Publishing is a hybrid publishing company dedicated to serving female authors. Our passion is to give voice, credibility and influence to authors with a mission and purpose of expanding their thought leadership and impact through published works.

Women Taking Charge Series

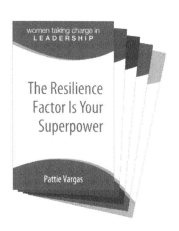

The Women Taking Charge series is a short-read book designed to elevate credibility, influence, and impact for subject matter experts. The series is focused on leadership, business, the workplace, life, and money.

52 Tips Series

The 52 Tips series is a concise, powerful tips book designed to elevate credibility, influence, and impact for subject matter experts on a variety of subjects or themes.

If you've always dreamed of writing a book and becoming a published author, let us support you and translate your expertise, passion, thoughts and wisdom into a published book!

Contact us to schedule a no-obligation book discovery session for *your* big book idea!

www.womenleadpublishing.com
800-591-1676

Made in the USA
Columbia, SC
12 August 2018